SERGEI O. PROKOFIEFF (1954–2014) studied Fine Arts and Painting at the Moscow School of Art. He encountered the work of Rudolf Steiner in his youth, and quickly decided to devote his life to it. He became active as an author and lecturer in 1982, and helped found the Anthroposophical Society in his native Russia in 1991. In Easter 2001, he was appointed as a member of the Executive Council of the General Anthroposophical Society in Dornach, Switzerland, a position he held until his death. A popular speaker, he wrote numerous books and articles that are published in many languages.

I0794708

Books by Sergei O. Prokofieff from Temple Lodge Publishing:

Anthroposophy and The Philosophy of Freedom
The Appearance of Christ in the Etheric
Crisis in the Anthroposophical Society and Pathways to the Future (with Peter Selg)
The Cycle of the Seasons and the Seven Liberal Arts
The Cycle of the Year as a Path of Initiation
The East in the Light of the West, Parts One to Three
The Encounter with Evil and its Overcoming through Spiritual Science
The Esoteric Significance of Spiritual Work in Anthroposophical Groups
Eternal Individuality, Towards a Karmic Biography of Novalis
The Foundation Stone Meditation
The Guardian of the Threshold and The Philosophy of Freedom
The Heavenly Sophia and the Living Being Anthroposophia
May Human Beings Hear It!, The Mystery of the Christmas Conference
The Mystery of John the Baptist and John the Evangelist
The Mystery of the Resurrection in the Light of Anthroposophy
The Occult Significance of Forgiveness
Prophecy of the Russian Epic
Relating to Rudolf Steiner
Riddle of the Human 'I'
Rudolf Steiner and the Founding of the New Mysteries
Rudolf Steiner's Path of Initiation
Rudolf Steiner's Research into Karma
Rudolf Steiner's Sculptural Group
The Spiritual Origins of Eastern Europe and the Future Mysteries of the Holy Grail
The Twelve Holy Nights and the Spiritual Hierarchies
What is Anthroposophy?
The Whitsun Impulse
Why Become a Member of the Anthroposophical Society?
Why Become a Member of the School of Spiritual Science?

The Case of Valentin Tomberg
Valentin Tomberg, Rudolf Steiner and Anthroposophy

The Esoteric Significance of Spiritual Work in Anthroposophical Groups and the Future of the Anthroposophical Society

SERGEI O. PROKOFIEFF

TEMPLE LODGE

Translated from Russian by Simon Blaxland-de Lange

Temple Lodge Publishing
Hillside House, The Square
Forest Row, RH18 5ES

www.templelodge.com

Published by Temple Lodge 2007

A catalogue record for this book is available from the British Library

ISBN 978 1902636 83 2

Cover by Andrew Morgan
Typeset by DP Photosetting, Neath, West Glamorgan
Printed and bound by 4edge Limited, UK

Contents

Foreword

The present extended essay consists of an expanded and more detailed version of a lecture that I gave at Rudolf Steiner House in London on 7 May 2006 on the occasion of the Annual General Meeting of the Anthroposophical Society in Great Britain.

At the request of certain friends who were present at the lecture, I have set it down in written form in order that it might be published in the *Newsletter*. In the course of this task the text of the transcript was supplemented by a series of thoughts, constituting further aspects of the lecture's basic theme, which could not—because of time constraints—be included in the lecture itself and were therefore omitted.

Nevertheless, their inclusion in the present complete text seems to me to be important, inasmuch as this is important for an overall understanding and further deepening of the general content of the lecture.

Moreover, while working on the written transcript I came to the conclusion that those portions of Rudolf Steiner's written works and lectures which were mentioned in my lecture—and which represented its spiritual-scientific foundation—must now, where possible, be quoted *verbatim*. This would enable the reader to continue to work independently with the themes touched upon in the lecture.

Such a decision did, however, give rise to the consequence that the text became considerably longer; and this—together with the additional aspects already referred to—has led to the substance of the lecture being presented not in the form of an article but as a separate booklet.

Sergei O. Prokofieff
Dornach, Trinity 2006

1. The Karma of the Anthroposophical Society

The Anthroposophical Society occupies an important place among the various spiritual and religious associations that exist everywhere in our time. Perhaps one of its most important qualities is the fact that Rudolf Steiner imparted to it a karma with respect to its founding and its subsequent spiritual activity of such a form and scope that is altogether without precedent or comparison among the spiritual movements of mankind.

In lectures that he gave on this theme it is particularly striking that Rudolf Steiner spoke in this connection again and again about the karma of the Anthroposophical Society as such and not only of the anthroposophical movement, which in itself would have been more understandable. No, he turned quite specifically to the members of the Anthroposophical Society actually existing on Earth, that is, to those anthroposophists who had made the spiritual decision to unite themselves with it, in order to define its karma and—with it—the karma of its founder. Thus, for example, in Arnhem (Holland) Rudolf Steiner prefaced what he had to say about his karma research with these words: 'I want to speak about something that has to do with the karma of the Anthroposophical Society itself' (GA 240, 18 July 1924).*

One of the deep mysteries of the Christmas Conference, when the General Anthroposophical Society was founded, is the fact that it was then that Rudolf Steiner united himself with it also with regard to his own karma, thus enabling him during the ensuing six months to reveal to the members of the Society not only their karma but also his own in connection with the heavenly antecedents of anthroposophy.[1]

For prior to its coming to Earth in the spiritual-scientific form in which it was founded by Rudolf Steiner in the first quarter of the 20th century, its essential nature was prepared in the spiritual worlds through two supersensible events, the description of which stands at the focus of all that Rudolf Steiner said about the karma of the Anthroposophical Society.

---

* For details of English translations, see Bibliography on p. 55.

Rudolf Steiner characterised the first and fundamental event as the all-embracing Michael School in the supersensible world, or, to be more precise, in the Sun sphere, where Michael himself over the course of several centuries taught the human souls connected with him who were at that time in his Sun sphere, together with a whole series of hierarchic beings and a large number of elemental spirits.

Rudolf Steiner presented the content of this teaching in a particularly detailed way in the lecture of 20 July 1924 in Arnhem. According to this lecture, at the heart of the teaching of the Michael School was a mighty metamorphosis of the old mystery wisdom into a 'great initiation-teaching' (GA 240, 20 July 1924), which must subsequently become the foundation for the new Christian mysteries. And as Rudolf Steiner spoke with respect to the cosmic activity of the Michael School of the arising of a new 'cosmic Christianity' (GA 240, 21 August 1924), it follows that the spiritual power whence Michael was able to accomplish the transformation of the ancient wisdom into a new Christianity was the power streaming into the whole of earthly evolution from the Mystery of Golgotha.

After this first stage of the heavenly preparation of anthroposophy, lasting from the end of the 14th to the beginning of the 18th century, a second stage in its cosmic development took place. It occurred not in the high Sun sphere but in the immediate spiritual surroundings of the Earth, and lasted not three centuries but in all several decades, from the end of the 18th until the beginning of the 19th century. Moreover, the entire character of this second stage was altogether different in nature. No longer would one be speaking of a Sun School but of a cosmic cultus, where the essential content of what Michael had imparted in his School was re-worked in mighty spiritual imaginations.

Rudolf Steiner connects also this supersensible cultus with the subsequent forming of 'the new Christianity' (GA 240, 18 July 1924) in the spiritual world, which follows from the fact that not only human souls participated in this event but also certain hierarchic beings and elemental spirits who had hitherto taken part in the Sun School. Thus both in the teaching of the supersensible School and in the subsequent re-working of its content in the cosmic cultus, at its heart was the central Christian Mystery that lies at the foundation not only of earthly but, above all, of 'heavenly' anthroposophy. Thus 'Michael placed before those who belonged to him the picture of cosmic relationships, the anthroposophical relationships. These souls received a teaching which unveiled the secrets of worlds' (GA 240, 20 July 1924), at the heart of which was the secret of the Mystery of Golgotha, as the focus of a 'new Christianity'.

This is the reason why certain people on Earth yearn for anthroposophy, and, once having encountered it, find in it the highest purpose of their lives. For 'whoever really has the impulse towards anthroposophy . . . still bears in his soul the echoes, the after-echoes of the fact that in the circle of Michael he received that *heavenly anthroposophy* which preceded the earthly. For the teachings given at that time by Michael were intended to prepare for what is now to become anthroposophy on Earth' (GA 237, 28 July 1924).

The relationship of human souls towards anthroposophy was formed in a different way through their participation in the supersensible cultus. Whereas in the Sun School of Michael they were essentially, so to speak, 'listeners' to the cosmic wisdom that was being imparted to them, in the course of the fulfilment of the cultus they were themselves able to take part in it, independently forming new cosmic imaginations from the content of the Michael School which they had made their own and weaving them into a fabric of all-embracing cultic activity.

As a result of this, the substance of the supersensible cultus was able to permeate their souls right down to the foundations of their will-nature, thereby enabling them to receive a new impulse into their souls which, after their incarnation on Earth, manifested itself in the capacity to develop an initiative emanating from anthroposophy. Rudolf Steiner described this quality of all true anthroposophists in the following words: 'This is indeed written in the karma of every single anthroposophist: Be a person of initiative . . . This should stand written in golden letters, constantly before the soul of the anthroposophist—that initiative lies in his karma, and that much of what meets him in life will depend on the extent to which he can become willingly, actively conscious of this initiative' (GA 237, 4 August 1924). By the word 'initiative' here what is meant is not only its outward manifestation, as expressed in some kind of practical activity, but also various kinds of inner initiative, for example, an active meditative life.

But in any case every anthroposophist must somewhere find a realm for bringing his initiative into being. For this yearning is so deeply part of his nature that, according to Rudolf Steiner, his entire living inner experience of his own life as fulfilled or as a failure, even to the extent of his health or illness, is dependent upon this possibility of giving rise to an initiative deriving from anthroposophy.

It can also be said: if through the teaching we have received in the School of Michael we seek anthroposophy on Earth, in order to link ourselves again on Earth with that stream of spiritual development upon which we embarked under Michael's leadership in his supersensible School, we bear within us through our participation in the imaginative cultus an impulse for earthly activity springing from anthroposophy. We want to create something new in the world upon its foundation.

Such thoughts are already doubtless familiar to the majority of anthroposophists, inasmuch as Rudolf Steiner spoke about this many times in his karma lectures. What is, perhaps, less well known is one particular fact of which Rudolf Steiner spoke on only one occasion but which, nevertheless, transforms the whole process described above into a harmonious whole that is complete in itself. This has to do with an event which took place in the spiritual worlds at the beginning of the 15th century, that is, when the Michael School had just begun its activity in the sphere of the Sun.

2. The Cosmic Thunderstorm

Rudolf Steiner described this cosmic event on one single occasion, in the lecture of 28 July 1924. At the time of this event the sublime First Hierarchy of the Seraphim, Cherubim and Thrones, which alone in the circle of the Hierarchies has such a spiritual power as to be able to imprint spiritual impulses upon matter itself,[2] directed the substance of cosmic thoughts (the Cosmic Intelligence) from the sphere of the Second, Sun Hierarchy of the Kyriotetes, Dynamis and Exusiai down to the Earth, in order with its help to transform the entire inner constitution of earthly human beings. The essence of this transformation was that man, who had hitherto been a 'being of the heart', henceforth became a 'being of the head'.

Of course, for many such a transformation of man on the part of the Hierarchies does not appear very attractive. Most people today would rather be beings of the heart than of the head. However, if one rightly understands this process it transpires that through such a change in human nature the path to the heart becomes for the first time in earthly evolution truly free and fully conscious. For man as a 'being of the heart' was in the past still fully dependent in the sphere of his feeling on the divine-spiritual Hierarchies who have guided him from ancient times, whereas having become a 'being of the head' he has been conclusively freed from their guardianship. The reason for this is that man's earthly thinking, inasmuch as it is associated with the physiological processes of the brain, is a dead thinking to which the Hierarchies no longer have any access. Hence only in the sphere of such a dead thinking is man able to arrive at an experience of his freedom.

With feeling, things stand quite differently. In the process of earthly evolution feeling has only partially become imbued with death-forces, which is why it has to a certain extent remained connected with the Hierarchies. Hence in the realm of feeling man does not possess total freedom. Still less is this possible in the realm of the will, where—in a condition of deep sleep—he has hitherto been inseparably connected with the spiritual Hierarchies who guide him, forming his karma in the depths of the will.

In contrast, once he has attained freedom in the realm of thinking as a 'being of the head', man can now enter freely and consciously into the sphere of the heart, in order gradually to transform it into a new organ of spiritual knowledge. (Subsequently he will be able to achieve this also with regard to his will and thereby arrive at a conscious experience of his karma.) For true heart-thinking, as an altogether new spiritual capacity, has become possible amongst mankind only after man's entire nature was changed by the First Hierarchy in the manner described.

Rudolf Steiner characterises this new path from the head to the heart as one towards which Michael now wants to direct man: 'He liberates thoughts from the sphere of the head; he clears the way for them to the heart' (GA 26, 'At the Dawn of the Michael Age'). For it is through thinking with the heart that a conscious collaboration between man and Michael is possible.

This enables one to understand those colossal changes in the historical development of humanity which took place on Earth as a result of this event. Academic history refers in this connection to a so-called 'modern age' beginning approximately in the early 15th century, while spiritual science speaks of the beginning of the consciousness-soul epoch (1413). It is even possible to say that the transformation within man by the First Hierarchy precisely at this time was a necessary precondition for the development on Earth of the consciousness soul.

The fact that the substance of cosmic thoughts that is necessary for such a transformation of human nature was drawn by the First Hierarchy from the sphere of activity of the Second, that is, directly from the Sun sphere, where at that very time the Michael School was beginning its activity, is an indication of its direct participation in this cosmic event. Rudolf Steiner said in this regard that at that time Michael, the hierarchic beings connected with him and human souls were direct witnesses of this cosmic event. However, in the spiritual world the very act of contemplating events taking place within it is a kind of participation in their arising. For those who witness them preserve in their being a 'memory' of what has taken place, which can then work further as a new creative impulse in their own deeds.

In one of the karma lectures given by Rudolf Steiner in England, he spoke of how in the supersensible School there participated, as pupils of Michael, not only a large circle of human souls who were at that time between death and a new birth but also a whole series of beings belonging to all three ranks of the Third Hierarchy: 'All the discarnate souls belonging to Michael took part in this great School in the supersensible world during the 14th, 15th and 16th centuries. All the beings of the Hierarchy of Angels, Archangels and Archai who belonged to the Michael stream, as well as many elemental beings, took part in it' (GA 240, 27 August 1924).

From this it follows that alongside human beings and numerous elemental spirits,[3] these beings belonging to the Third Hierarchy were also supersensible witnesses of the transformation of human nature referred to brought about by the forces of the First and Second Hierarchy. Furthermore, in a certain sense it is even possible to speak of their participation in this event, as in the spiritual worlds—especially if one is speaking about hierarchic beings—even the contemplation of an event is a definite form of participation in it. Thus it is possible to say that in the process of the spiritual transformation of man's being that took place at the beginning of the 15th century all *nine* Hierarchies were present, albeit in a completely different way.

Rudolf Steiner describes what was then revealed to the spiritual sight of the participants in the Michael School from the Sun sphere as a mighty spiritual thunderstorm, which broke out at that time in the surroundings of the Earth as a reflection of the mighty activity of the First Hierarchy, impressing upon earthly human beings the substance of the Cosmic Intelligence from the realm of the Second Hierarchy: 'One sees the Seraphim, Cherubim and Thrones bearing the spiritual from the realm of the Exusiai, Dynamis and Kyriotetes down into the physical, and by their power implanting the spiritual into the physical... The Seraphim, Cherubim and Thrones were carrying over the Cosmic Intelligence into that member of man's organisation which we call the system of nerves and senses, the head-organisation ... Formerly man was a heart-man; since then he became a head-man. The Intelligence becomes his own' (GA 237, 28 July 1924).

On the Earth, however—despite the immense changes in human culture and history that began to follow from this time onwards—human beings hardly noticed any of the spiritual events taking place around them and *within them*. Only in the esoteric schools of true

Rosicrucians strictly hidden from the outer world did there exist knowledge about this cosmic thunderstorm and the subsequent transformation of human nature. (Ibid.)

In this connection Rudolf Steiner refers to a further fact of considerable importance which directly concerns anthroposophists themselves. For if they, as participants in the Michael School and—hence—as direct witnesses of the events described, try to immerse themselves sufficiently deeply in their own souls to the point where there awaken *memories* of their experience of the heavenly thunderstorm, these memories will be able to serve them as a source of true anthroposophical enthusiasm: 'This should be understood, my dear friends, for these thunders and lightnings must become enthusiasm in the hearts and minds of anthroposophists!' (Ibid.).

This enthusiasm can be experienced especially strongly through immersing ourselves intensively in anthroposophical ideas, which then become for us a kind of memory-process with regard to what we ourselves apprehended in the supersensible Michael School. For such spiritual enthusiasm as wells up from the depths of the soul in the process of studying anthroposophy is none other than a first conscious approach to our own anthroposophical karma, to our true affinity with the supersensible stream of Michael in the higher worlds with which we were connected before we entered earthly existence.

Thus if in recent times one hears again and again in anthroposophical circles the opinion that work in anthroposophical groups or branches has become outdated, that the study of anthroposophical ideas (naturally not only with the head but also with the heart, that is, not in an abstract, intellectual way but livingly, so that in the process of study the whole person participates) no longer calls forth enthusiasm but, in contrast, is with increasing frequency experienced as a burden which one needs to bear out of tradition, out of a 'debt of service' or in consequence of other considerations, this signifies none other than that we have steadily been distancing ourselves from our anthroposophical karma. We have tragically begun to forget those resolves which we ourselves made as pupils of Michael in his supersensible School and then brought down into the depths of our will in the imaginative cultus, in order that we might become on Earth his true servants, endeavouring out of freedom to implement not only our will but—above all—*his* will with respect to the further evolution of mankind.

On the other hand, if we have been able so to enliven and deepen our inner experience of anthroposophical ideas that they are capable of inspiring us with real enthusiasm and a joy of knowledge, filling our life with new light and meaning, this signifies that—on coming to Earth—we have been able to form a connection with our Michaelic karma and that we now on this foundation wish to work further with it in the sense that will be described in what follows.

Moreover, only such a karmically engendered experience of a genuine spiritual enthusiasm with respect to anthroposophical work represents a solid foundation for establishing a new human community. For this enthusiasm is then the motivating power behind that spiritual idealism which is necessary for bringing into being the 'reversed cultus' when carrying out anthroposophical work together. Rudolf Steiner was referring to this when he addressed anthroposophists in direct speech: 'When you imbue your inner being with will and *infuse it with enthusiasm*, you are conveying your idealised sense experience in a direction exactly opposite to that taken when you embody the supersensible in the ritual of the cultus' (GA 257, 27 February 1923). Of such a nature is the path leading to the reversed cultus. Through it we can indeed raise ourselves to the spheres of the Hierarchies and so embark upon the implementing of the task which Rudolf Steiner formulated as follows: 'Human beings must work together with the Gods, with Michael himself' (GA 240, 19 July 1924).

The source of this new enthusiasm can also be understood from another point of view. When we study anthroposophy, we first learn to make use of that wholly new capacity which humanity did not as yet possess in the past, namely, to *understand with earthly reason* the processes, events and beings of the spiritual world with a similar exactitude of thinking and well-nigh mathematical clarity as, from the modern age onwards, scientists have investigated and gained knowledge of outer nature and its laws. Until the appearance on Earth of anthroposophy, such a possibility for humanity did not exist. But if we ask ourselves about its sources, we shall have inwardly to take ourselves to the Sun and, as we look from thence to the Earth, experience in its surroundings the mighty 'spiritual thunderstorm' as a reflection of that radical change in human nature through which the appearance on Earth of anthroposophy and its comprehension by every healthy human intellect (the first stage of modern initiation[4]) became possible.

Thus if we study anthroposophy and do not baulk at any difficulties, we do actually awaken within ourselves this wholly new capacity which can be developed only in our time, that is, in the course of the present epoch of the Time Spirit Michael's rulership amongst mankind; as in future, once it has come to an end—and it will continue to last for three to four centuries—the tasks of humanity will become different and it will be difficult to make up for what has not been achieved.

To summarise what has been presented so far, one can say that the heavenly preparation of anthroposophy passed through not two but *three* stages. The first of these from a temporal point of view was the 'spiritual thunderstorm' with the subsequent transformation of human nature which, from an occult point of view, was what made the dawning on Earth of the consciousness-soul epoch at all possible. There then followed the Michael School in the Sun sphere over several centuries and then, finally, the whole process concluded with the imagination-based cultus in the spiritual world nearest to the Earth.

3. Spiritual Pre-History

Before continuing with the main thread of the present essay, it is necessary to consider the occult 'pre-history' of that event through which man made the transition from a 'heart-being' to a 'head-being' at the threshold of the modern age. Rudolf Steiner indicated in this connection that events of such a kind occur extremely rarely in earthly evolution. The previous one took place in ancient Atlantis. 'It was in the Atlantean time that such a thing had last manifested itself, as seen from the aspect of the supersensible' (GA 237, 28 July 1924).

It follows from these words that in the case in question we can speak about a definite rhythm encompassing vast periods of earthly evolution, periods which Rudolf Steiner, in the early lectures where he still used theosophical terminology, called 'root races'. On the basis of the character of the last event described above, it is possible to draw the conclusion that on ancient Atlantis the whole of nature was similarly transformed by the combined activity of the First and Second Hierarchies at that time in such a way that man was transformed from a 'limb-being' into a 'heart-being'.

Tracing this evolution further into the past, one may suppose that a still earlier event in this series took place on ancient Lemuria. This first event in the sequence consisted in that the Sun substance of the Cosmic Intelligence from the realm of the Second Hierarchy was at that time first inculcated into man by the beings of the First Hierarchy.

Thus in all we have three successive cosmic events. On ancient Lemuria the substance of the Sun Intelligence first entered into man and permeated initially only his limb system. On Atlantis it was elevated by the Hierarchies to the level above and permeated the heart system; while in the post-Atlantean period, on the threshold of the consciousness-soul epoch, during which the foundation for the successful conclusion of earthly evolution had to be laid, the Cosmic Intelligence was introduced into man's head system.[5]

What has just been said can shed a new light on the fact that it was during Lemuria that humanity was endowed with an individual ego, the substance of which was sacrificed by the Spirits of Form, or to be more precise by the seven Sun Elohim spoken of in the Bible. Thus it was in the course of the permeation at that time of man's limbs by the Sun Intelligence that the substance of his ego could also enter in.

And then through the second cosmic event, on ancient Atlantis, this ego-substance was elevated to man's heart system; while at the beginning of the 15th century it was raised to the head region, as a result of which man's entire being (all of his three systems) was for the first time permeated by the ego impulse. In this way the foundation was laid for his experiencing himself as a free ego-being, as had to come about in the epoch of the consciousness soul.

In a surprising way all three developmental stages that have been described are repeated in a microcosmic and accelerated form in the (ordinary) process of waking up. Even a purely outward observation can show that in the process of waking the ego and astral body return to the physical and etheric sheaths, passing as they do through three stages. This is manifested outwardly in that, immediately before a person wakes up, as a rule he makes some involuntary movements with his limbs or with his whole body, then opens his eyes or, before opening them, begins dimly to apprehend the sounds, light and temperature around him, while only with the beginning of mental activity can waking be regarded as having fully happened.

These three stages of waking correspond to the penetration of the ego first into man's limbs, then into his rhythmic system and, finally, his head system.[6] At the first of these stages there is a repetition of the event in the Lemurian epoch, when man was endowed with the ego principle; at the second stage there is a repetition of the event in the Atlantean period, in the course of which man for the first time set foot on solid earthly soil from the atmospheric surroundings of the Earth, as a result of which his eyes and other sense-organs for apprehending the outer world were opened. And finally, from the 15th century onwards, man arrived at the experience that he produces his thoughts himself and does not receive them as inspirations from the spiritual world. In other words, from this time man's intellectual activity was wholly united with the physiological processes of his brain, as a result of which his thoughts took on the character of shadowy (dead) images, in whose spectral world the experience of individual freedom became possible.

4. The Threefold Source of Karma

As we have seen, all nine Hierarchies took part in the three stages of the heavenly forming of anthroposophy, especially in its very first stage. Thus they are all in one way or another associated with the developmental process of the *karma* of the anthroposophical movement.

Thus in order to proceed further, we need to ask ourselves what this karma actually is, and in a broader sense about karma in general. An ordinary answer to this question would run as follows: karma is a law of cause and effect in the moral structure of the world, or a law of universal justice working from one incarnation to another. But such a definition of karma is very abstract. If one considers its reality in the spiritual world, its essential nature can be discerned in this way: 'This human karma, at first, is like a veil, a curtain. If we look behind this veil, we gaze at the weaving deeds and influences of Archai, Archangeloi, Angeloi; Kyriotetes, Dynamis, Exusiai; Seraphim, Cherubim, Thrones' (GA 239, 8 June 1924).

The influence of all three (nine) Hierarchies in the process of forming human karma can be characterised in the following way. The Third Hierarchy (Angeloi, Archangeloi, Archai)—the Hierarchy closest to man—constantly transfers the karma created by human beings to the spiritual world, where it is transmitted to the beings of the Second Hierarchy (Exusiai, Dynamis, Kyriotetes), who transform it in such a way that it can be united with the entire spiritual cosmos. Finally, the First Hierarchy (Thrones, Cherubim, Seraphim) draws the consequences of what has become world karma back down to the earthly world, where it imprints it right into earthly matter, so that its consequences meet the person concerned in his next incarnation in accordance with the natural laws prevailing on Earth.

One can also say: the Third Hierarchy bears within itself full *consciousness* of all the karmic connections of earthly human beings. The Second Hierarchy imbues them with the *life* of the spiritual cosmos, while the First Hierarchy gives them that firm and final *form* in which they then work on Earth as the laws of a higher, divine justice.

According to the Foundation Stone Meditation the nine Hierarchies are not merely divided into three categories in accordance with the three aspects of the hierarchic beings in each, but are also successively connected with the three persons of the Holy Trinity. The First Hierarchy is connected with the being of the Divine Father, the Second with that of the Son or Christ, and the Third with the being of the Holy Spirit. From this it follows that also in the realm of karma it is necessary for us, in accordance with the archetypal picture of the Foundation Stone Meditation, to distinguish three kinds of karmic effects. Firstly there is the way that karma works out of the forces of the Father through the First Hierarchy of Seraphim, Cherubim and Thrones, then the effect that it has out of the forces of the Son or Christ through the Second, Sun Hierarchy of Kyriotetes, Dynamis and Exusiai, and, finally, the working of the karma-forming forces of the Holy Spirit through the mediation of the beings of the Third Hierarchy, the Archai, Archangels and Angels.

The difference between these three aspects of karma can be represented as follows. The Father impulse always acts in the sphere of karma with the force of natural necessity. Here the person concerned is unable to change anything. It is merely given to him to receive and bear this karma even if it is associated with hard blows of destiny and great suffering. To this aspect of karma belong incurable diseases and accidents. It is not unusual for karma of this nature to play a part—also in a positive sense—in encounters between people. Let us take an example. Two individuals, one from Berlin and the other from New Zealand, meet for the first time at a bus-stop in the middle of London. Their meeting is calculated to the second, as a moment later the bus would already have departed, taking one of them away, and their meeting would not have taken place.

If we now take into consideration that as a result of such a 'chance' encounter the destiny of the one, and perhaps of both of them, changes quite fundamentally (for example, through this acquaintance one of them meets with anthroposophy, or perhaps a friendship arises from this meeting and possibly also family ties for one's whole life), then as they survey their past lives both participants are able to show how from early childhood onwards a whole series of greater and lesser events led to the meeting in London at the bus-stop taking place many years later. As a result an awareness may arise of an infinitely deep secret wisdom that works in human life beyond consciousness and leads to events of the kind described above. And one could cite many such events in ordinary life.

The forces of the Son work altogether differently in the sphere of karma. Here, as we have seen, it is a question of transforming karma, that is, metamorphosing it. For once—in the example cited—two people, who are known through their past karma, have met one another, it depends on their freedom what they do with this meeting. One can say that now their essential task is to transform past karma into future karma. An example may make this clear.

An anthroposophist who had major problems with his wife once came to Rudolf Steiner for advice. Living together seemed to him to be impossible and he wanted to know whether it would be better to separate from her than to go on tormenting one another. Rudolf Steiner's response was: 'It is better to bring this karma into order in this life, since in the next one it will be even harder'. To be sure, the answer that he gave concerned mainly one particular situation and should not be applied mechanically to all similar ones; but nevertheless there is the clear indication that precisely in such difficult situations it is a question of working consciously on the transformation of karma.

The influence exerted on the sphere of karma by the forces of the Holy Spirit is far more difficult to characterise, since processes are involved which are still only at the very beginning of their development amongst mankind. Thus in ordinary life we are capable of taking only very few steps in this direction. What concerns us here are actions which do not have any previous karma and, hence, represent something wholly new in earthly evolution. Here everything depends upon human freedom and inner initiative. Man has to learn in a certain sense to 'create out of nothing' and, through this, work on the foundation of an altogether new karma.

In our time of the etheric appearance of Christ, He works in the forming of all three aspects of karma, though in different ways. In the sphere of influence of the karmic forces of the Father, Christ appears as the Comforter, helping people to bear the burden of the karma which it is impossible to change within the confines of a particular earthly life. From His own sphere Christ works today as the Lord of Karma, that is, as a spiritual Helper guiding a person in the balancing out of his karma in such a way that the fruits of this individual work may serve the greatest good for the whole of humanity (see GA 130, 2 December 1911). Finally, through the influence of the forces of the Holy Spirit in the sphere of the forming of karma we can ourselves become Christ's collaborators in the process of creating a new cosmos.

In this sense the growth of anthroposophy on Earth represents a stream of development which passes through three successive stages. From the exposition of anthroposophy as modern spiritual science in the strictly intellectual form of *Occult Science*, it evolves into the forms and colours of the First Goetheanum, where the entire substance of anthroposophy becomes a visible imaginative picture. And when the Goetheanum passed in the element of fire into the spiritual world, Rudolf Steiner was able to apprehend its impulse in a wholly transformed way out of the far reaches of the cosmos and then return it to Earth as the 'esoteric impulse' of the Christmas Conference (see GA 233a, 22 April 1924).

This entire development was at the same time associated with the revelation of the mysteries of karma, which was Rudolf Steiner's principal life's task.[7] The teaching about karma, encompassing not only the development of human beings as they pass through a succession of earthly incarnations, but also the evolution of the karma of the cosmos, connected as it is with the activity of the higher Hierarchies and manifested in the evolutionary stages of our universe from Old Saturn to Vulcan, was given a firm foundation in the book *Occult Science*; while in the First Goetheanum this spiritual-scientific substance appeared in artistic forms and colours, calling forth within man the faculty of karmic vision. (See GA 236, 27 April 1924.) Finally, at the Christmas Conference a new esoteric impulse was given to the Anthroposophical Society, enabling its members consciously to approach practical work on their own karma. The karma lectures, together with their culmination of the revelation of the karma of the Anthroposophical Society itself, were intended to serve as the foundation for this task.

On the basis of what has been said, it is not difficult to see that in the three stages of the supersensible preparation of anthroposophy as described above we have a steady process of preparation of a particular group of human souls for subsequently understanding the threefold working of karma in earthly life.

Thus the cosmic deed described by Rudolf Steiner as a 'cosmic thunderstorm' represents the working of karma from the sphere of the Father in, one could say, an especially typical form. Here a spiritual impulse deriving from the sphere of the First Hierarchy, with a power of the highest natural necessity and lying wholly outside the earthly consciousness of human beings, profoundly altered man's nature with regard to the supersensible parts of his physical organism. To express the point in earthly language, no-one has actually asked man what he thinks about this and whether he agrees with such a cardinal change in his entire inner being.

In contrast, in the supersensible Michael School what was happening was, as we have seen, a mighty metamorphosis wrought by Michael out of the forces of the Mystery of Golgotha with respect to the transforming of the nature of old mysteries into the new mysteries. Thus here we have the source of those forces that we need on Earth in order consciously to work on our past karma, transforming it into future karma. For the karma of the ancient mysteries is inseparably connected with our own karma in past incarnations.

Finally, in the supersensible cultus we received into ourselves, down to the will regions of our being, a spiritual power that gives rise on Earth to the capacity to manifest activity and initiative also in the realm of karma. This signifies the beginning of the free and conscious creation of a wholly new karma, with a significance not only for human beings on Earth but also for the Hierarchies in the spiritual world.

5. Work with Karma and the Foundation Stone Meditation

All three forms of karmic influence can also be found in the Foundation Stone Meditation, inasmuch as it contains, in seed-form, all that was to be developed by Rudolf Steiner on the foundation of the esoteric impulse of the Christmas Conference. Among these spiritual fruits of the Christmas Conference are, first and foremost, the new revelations from the sphere of karma contained in the karma lectures of 1924.

The first part of the Meditation concerns the working of the forces of the Father through the mediation of the First Hierarchy, begetting new being in depths of worlds:

For the Father-spirit of the heights holds sway
In depths of worlds begetting being.

Of course, this creation of new existence by the highest hierarchic beings can only refer to their working in the earthly world with the power of natural necessity, exclusive of any influence on this process on the part of any beings of a lower status, including man.

An altogether different mood meets us in the second part of the Meditation. Here it is a question of the influence of the Son or Christ in the Earth's surroundings, where His will has held sway since the Mystery of Golgotha. However, it is directed not towards the creating of existence but towards the further development of human souls. In the 'rhythms of worlds', that is, in the manifold processes of soul and spiritual metamorphosis, Christ leads human beings to a full realisation of their karma, that is, to a conscious transformation in the sense of the aims and tasks of the earthly maturation of humanity. Even the very expression the 'will of Christ' is an indication of the relationship of this process with the essential nature of karma, for in human nature the forces of karma work above all in the unconscious depths of man's will, where the Christ is present as the Lord of Karma.

And if a human being of today really embarks in full consciousness on working on his past karma, that is, on its transformation into the karma of the future, the Christ will be beside him, helping him to carry out this task in such a way that it may serve the greatest good of all people. When this comes about, when the balancing out of individual karma under the influence of the power of Christ becomes an impulse promoting the further development and spiritualisation of the whole of mankind, it is indeed possible to speak about the 'grace' emanating from Christ as the Lord of Karma, making human souls capable of working on their own karma for the good of earthly evolution as a whole.

> For the Christ-Will in the encircling round [of the Earth] holds sway
> In the rhythms of the worlds, bestowing grace on the soul.

In this karma-forming activity of Christ the spirits of the Second, Sun Hierarchy participate, serving Him in the higher worlds.

The movement of the Sun from East to West described in this part of the Meditation:

> Let there be fired from the East
> What through the West is formed

is also a reference to the working of Sun forces in earthly evolution as the principal source not only of natural but also all soul-spiritual metamorphoses.

The third part of the Meditation refers in no less clear a way to the creation of new karma. What is being spoken of here is something that arises for the first time on Earth out of the free deeds of man, but which has significance not only for human beings but also for the beings of the higher Hierarchies. Hence the fundamental gesture of the third part is not from above downwards, as in the first, and not from East to West, as in the second, but from below upwards, from the 'depths', from the world of earthly human beings up to the world of spirit, to the realm of activity of the heavenly Hierarchies.

> For the World-thoughts of the Spirit hold sway
> In the depths of the worlds, craving for light.

Thus a reference to human freedom is encountered only in this third part of the Meditation. But in combination with the word 'will' its influence also extends to the sphere of karma.

On thine own I
[Bestow]
For thy free willing.

For the first time in earthly evolution freedom and karma cease to be opposing forces, and in their collaboration they reveal to man the possibility of attaining a higher freedom precisely in the creation of new karma, which is possible for him only on Earth, that is—from a spiritual point of view—'in the depths of the world'.

What was already prepared at the previous stage through the participation of Christ in the transformation of human karma, but remained confined by the presence in this process—and by the influence upon it—of the karma of the past, becomes at the third stage an independent spiritual activity on the part of man in which there participate only those beings of the Third Hierarchy who are closest to him and who work in the spiritual worlds out of the impulse of the Holy Spirit.

Archai, Archangeloi, Angeloi!
Let there be prayed from the depths
What in the heights will be heard

Under the leadership of Michael as Time *Spirit*, who represents the forces of the Holy Spirit in the present epoch of his leadership of mankind, these beings of the Third Hierarchy bear the consequences of the new karma-creating deeds of human beings into the higher worlds, where they become the building stones of a new cosmos. (See the next chapter.)

In this connection the mentioning of the ego principle in all three parts of the Foundation Stone Meditation is full of special significance. In the first part it still wholly abides in the bosom of the forces of karmic necessity (world justice) that guide it, forces deriving from the sphere of the Father:

Thine own I
Abides [literally 'comes to being']
Within God's I.

In the second part what is spoken of is the free uniting of man's individual ego with the Christ impulse, as its cosmic archetype or 'World Ego':

> Thine own I
> Unite[s]
> With the World-I.

Finally, in the third part the human ego acquires not only full individual freedom but becomes capable of itself creating new existence out of this freedom. For this, however, it first has to gain an understanding of the 'World-Light', or—to use a more traditional phrase—the *Astral Light*, in which the 'eternal aims of Gods' relating to the whole of earthly evolution are revealed:

> On thine own I
> Bestow
> For thy free willing.

Only on the foundation of this knowledge, when in complete freedom man makes these 'eternal aims of Gods' his own aims in his ego, fulfilling them not as the alien intentions of other beings but in the sense of *The Philosophy of Freedom*—as *his own most intimate aims*, only then will he in full measure attain the possibility of collaborating with the Gods of the cosmos in the process of creating new karma.

In conclusion it is necessary to point out that the fourth part of the Meditation testifies to Christ's participation after the Mystery of Golgotha in all three aspects of karma, as described above: in the working of the karma of the Father, Christ is revealed to man as a Comforter; in the karma of the Son, as a Helper; in the karma of the Holy Spirit, as a Friend and Collaborator.

6. The Modern Mysteries of Michael

It should be striking to anyone who studies the substance of the Christmas Conference that Rudolf Steiner hardly ever mentioned the name of Michael.[8]

This initially apparently most puzzling fact is, however, explained in the lecture that Rudolf Steiner gave approximately twelve days after the end of the Christmas Conference, on the day when the Foundation Stone Meditation was published in the 'Supplement for Members' of the weekly journal *Das Goetheanum*. In this lecture Rudolf Steiner not only mentioned Michael's name as often as in any other lecture on this theme but also for the first time gave the entirely new image of the ruling Time Spirit. Subsequently, this image of Michael was to be developed at some length in the karma lectures.

The most important difference between Michael and all the other Archangels of his rank is that he is the only one in their circle who fully acknowledges man's freedom on the Earth. Hence in this lecture Rudolf Steiner calls him the 'spiritual hero of freedom' (GA 233a, 13 January 1924). Such a relationship of Michael to human freedom does, however, have consequences for him himself. In contrast to the other Archangels he has in our time become 'taciturn', a Time Spirit who gives human beings very little by way of directives, indications, inspirations and impulses for action. Whereas the other Archangels endeavour to continue to guide humanity by prompting individual people to carry out one or another deed, Michael almost wholly refrains from this, exhibiting as he does an interest not in the motives of human deeds but only in their consequences.

In other words, he gives a person the possibility of accomplishing something in the world springing from what he has acquired by way of spiritual-scientific knowledge and then judges the consequences of his deed from the standpoint of the spiritual world. Rudolf Steiner describes this process with the help of the following imagination. A person approaches Michael in the spiritual world with the consequences of his free deeds. This may take place through initiation, or after death, or also during sleep, whereby what is being described here applies today to all human individuals. Then Michael, not with words but with a glance and a gesture, enables the person to understand whether or not his deeds can be positively valued from the standpoint of the world rulership of the cosmos. Here Michael appears before the human individual not with a sword but with a pair of scales. And if his decision is a positive one, the person draws the interpretation: 'That is right, that is in harmony with the cosmic guidance' (GA 233a, 13 January 1924). Then Michael takes the consequences of the person's deeds into his domain, where his earthly deeds become cosmic deeds, that is, building stones of that new cosmos that has been spoken of above.[9]

However, in connection with what is said in the lecture referred to, there arises one significant question which—if not resolved satisfactorily—becomes a real problem. The fact is that Rudolf Steiner describes the free deeds of man which can be acknowledged by Michael in such a way that, in accomplishing them, man must be guided by what has been read in the astral light of the cosmos. But in order to learn to read in it, one needs oneself to become initiated, that is, attain a stage of individual development which for the overwhelming majority of anthroposophists lies as yet far in the future and will hardly be achieved by them in this life.

One could say—well then, they will achieve it in the next incarnation. But such an answer does not resolve the basic problem, inasmuch as the next incarnation of the majority of anthroposophists now living will come at a time which will follow *after* the end of the modern Michael epoch (it ends in two or three centuries). But Michael needs the free deeds of human beings resulting from the reading in the astral light already now, that is, in the epoch of his present rulership amongst mankind.

On the other hand, it is completely impossible to imagine that Rudolf Steiner would have presented anthroposophists with a task which was in principle beyond their capacity within the confines of a single earthly incarnation, in the knowledge that in the next incarnation it would already be too late. However, if one really ponders this riddle, the answer turns out to be far more accessible and obvious than one might have initially supposed. It is connected precisely with the fundamental nature of modern initiation, consisting as it does in that the person being initiated must, in the course of his spiritual research, not only be in a condition to read in the astral light but—in order to make the spiritual facts that he has discovered accessible to *all* human beings—must translate everything that he has read in the astral light into the language of modern thought and, hence, convey these facts to the minds of other human beings.

This cardinal distinctive quality of modern initiation, which is connected with Rudolf Steiner's essential task in his incarnation in the 20th century, was characterised by him in a conversation with Maria Röschl. Ernst Lehrs spoke of this in the following words: 'Maria Röschl once asked Rudolf Steiner whether in his time there was an initiate who could see as high and as far as he. As she told me later, his answer was: Indeed there is, but no-one who is able to clothe what he has seen in the form of thoughts that can enable others to reconstruct it in their own thinking. For that would necessitate conveying what has been perceived spiritually to the brain; and this is a sacrifice which no-one else would be able to make.'[10]

It follows from this that, from the moment when occult knowledge is conveyed by the initiate through his physical brain and thereby becomes thoughts that are generally accessible and comprehensible for mankind, there hardly any longer exists any difference in principle between an initiate and a non-initiate. Until this moment the basic difference between them lay in that only an initiate could investigate spiritual facts in the supersensible worlds (that is, reading in the astral light), and, moreover, not merely an initiate but one who had truly reached the heights of *modern* initiation, sacrificially allowing the supersensible knowledge that had been thus received to be drawn down into the physical brain in order to give it an intellectual form comprehensible to anyone.

If this had not been so, the rule repeated ever and again by Rudolf Steiner to the effect that only an initiate can, of course, engage in research in the spiritual world, whereas anyone with a healthy and unprejudiced power of reason is capable of understanding the results of his research, would not have any meaning. However, it is the application of this rule to the study of the results of true spiritual research which constitutes the first stage of the modern path of initiation, which Rudolf Steiner formulated as follows in *Occult Science*: 'The study of spiritual science, where one initially uses the sound judgement acquired in the physical world'(GA 13, p. 295).

It follows from this that in absorbing what is imparted by spiritual science, though not in an abstract, intellectual way but including our whole human nature with our feeling and will in the process of study, we are *already reading in the astral light*, even though not directly but through the mediation of modern spiritual-scientific thoughts. In which case, nothing is any longer hindering us from beginning to act in full freedom out of what has been read *in this way* (that is, through the mediation of earthly thinking) in the astral light. And this represents a path to the deeds which Michael expects from us at any time, if only we can relate so seriously to what is imparted by the modern initiate that we make the results of his spiritual research the motivating power of our actions.

Such actions as consequences of our own initiative deriving from a purely spiritual impulse, the capacity for which initiative was brought to our awareness thanks to our participation in the supersensible Michael cultus before our birth on Earth, thereby represent the foundation for the arising amongst mankind of a new karma that does not have a past and is therefore directed only towards the future. For the possibility of finding such a free and conscious relationship to the content of the spiritual world, as revealed in the astral light, before the arrival on Earth of spiritual science or anthroposophy was simply not available to humanity. Moreover, the consciousness and freedom in this process is guaranteed by the fact that the mediating element is thinking, through which man finds the highest stage of consciousness attainable on Earth and also approaches an experience of his freedom, springing as it does from what is the fundamental experience of a human being today, namely, that his thoughts are his own fully independent creation.

Thus the well-known words from the Gospel, 'Blessed are those who have not seen and yet believe' (John 20:29) spoken to the Apostle Thomas, as a representative of the future epoch of the consciousness soul, can in the light of modern initiation also be expressed as 'Blessed are those who have not seen and yet know'. In this sense those people are truly blessed who are working today in the world out of an anthroposophical knowledge of the spiritual worlds, for their deeds in creating a new karma can be received by Michael into the bosom of the Hierarchies as something which only man is able to unite with the universal hierarchic whole, crowning it with a new, radiant summit of achievement—the creative deeds of the Tenth Hierarchy.

7. The Esoteric Structure of the Anthroposophical Society

If one bears in mind that the fulfilment of karma is brought about between individual human beings, it becomes understandable why Rudolf Steiner, from the outset of his activity as a spiritual teacher, concerned himself not only about the individual development of his pupils in the sense of the path described in the book *Knowledge of the Higher Worlds* but also devoted immense efforts to organising throughout Europe individual groups for the common study of anthroposophy.

Especially at the Christmas Conference, Rudolf Steiner placed both aspects of man's spiritual activity—the individual and the social—at the centre of the process of the founding of the new mysteries. Thus the Foundation Stone Meditation, as their mantric expression, begins with a threefold addressing of the human soul ('Soul of man!') that is following the path of modern initiation and ends in the fourth part with a mighty call to the social unification of human beings, whose streams are rooted in the spiritual Sun of Christ: 'That good may become, what we . . .'.

The same can be said of the supersensible Foundation Stone forming the esoteric focus of the Christmas Conference. First it must be laid by man in the soil of his heart as a purely individual act, representing the consequence of a free resolve of his will. Subsequently, however, it grows and is revealed in the human heart no longer as the focus of individual development but as the supersensible foundation of a human community having the aim of consciously working on the forming of new karma.

Rudolf Steiner referred immediately after the Christmas Conference to this esoteric aim of the socially formative activity of the Anthroposophical Society which was so directly connected with his central task on the Earth. In answer to a question that he himself posed in one of the karma lectures: Why do people join the Anthroposophical Society?, he said: 'What is it in the last resort that unites the members of the Anthroposophical Society? It is that they are to bring order again into their karma ... They are striving once more to live and express their real karma. This is the cosmic ray that pours through the anthroposophical movement, clearly perceptible to one who knows. It is the restoration of the truth in karma. In this connection we can understand very much, both of the destiny of individuals in the Anthroposophical Society and of the destiny of the whole Society' (GA 237, 8 August 1924).

The need to bring earthly karma into order derives from the fact that, as a result of the separation of a whole group of Angels from the kingdom of Michael, the karma of mankind fell into disorder. Many catastrophic events of our time can be explained precisely in this way. (See the lecture quoted above.) Hence one of the most important tasks of the modern Michael epoch is working on karma, and not only between human beings but also between them and the beings of the Hierarchy closest to them. It was for this purpose (among many others, of course) that the General Anthroposophical Society was founded. And through a knowledge of one's own karma in connection with the cosmic stream of Michael (the three stages of the heavenly preparation of anthroposophy described above), the necessary foundation was given to the Society for the accomplishing of this task.

Here it is necessary to point out that such a task of creating new karma between human and spiritual beings concerns above all the beings of the Third Hierarchy, the closest to humanity and as the group souls leading mankind to the fulfilment of its earthly aims. Thus the Angels, in addition to their activity as Guardian Angels, are also the group souls of smaller groups of people, especially when these latter are interconnected by bonds of a spiritual kind or a shared spiritual task; the Archangels as group souls lead larger groups of people or, as Folk Spirits, whole nations; finally the Archai, in their capacity as group souls, embrace whole portions of mankind and also, as Time Spirits, humanity as a whole, guiding it for the duration of a particular period.

If from this standpoint one considers the esoteric structure of the Anthroposophical Society and what it became as a result of the Christmas Conference, it can be described in the following way.[11] From the very beginning of Rudolf Steiner's spiritual-scientific activity, anthroposophical work in groups or branches has been at the foundation of the Anthroposophical Society. In 1923, in preparing anthroposophists for the Christmas Conference, Rudolf Steiner himself referred to the esoteric foundations of this work. Through development in groups, in the process of studying spiritual science together or of a reversed cultus (the result of the inner awakening of those participating in such group work through the shared experiencing of the soul-spiritual nature of another person), a relationship can gradually be forged within them with the realm of the Angels: 'The anthroposophical community seeks to lift human souls into supersensible realms so that they may enter the company of Angels' (GA 257, 3 March 1923).

In other words, through the free, common activity of the participants of such a group, an altogether new possibility of collaborating with human beings is offered to the Angels. As new group souls, such Angels are then able to collaborate with anthroposophical groups in the process of their bringing about a 'reversed cultus'.

Similarly, the uniting of separate groups in a national society acquires from this standpoint a deeper, esoteric significance. It consists in that the anthroposophical groups combined within it gain the possibility of working with the sphere of the Archangels and, above all, with the Archangel who, as Folk Spirit, is connected with that particular country. The awareness of a common service to this Folk Spirit which unites the various groups also opens up access to a collaboration with other Archangels who are not Folk Spirits, and who are then able to work within such groups as new group souls of a higher order.

Hence in 1923, in the process of gradually preparing for the Christmas Conference, Rudolf Steiner visited various European countries in order to found national societies. And then at Christmas that same year, the representatives and members of the individual groups and national societies that had arisen by that time were invited to Dornach in order under Rudolf Steiner's leadership together to found the General—that is, universally human, and in this capacity independent of any national or racial affinity—Anthroposophical Society with its centre at the Goetheanum.

At the Christmas Conference Rudolf Steiner spoke of this in the following words: 'The suggestion had been made by me to found national Societies on the basis of which the General Anthroposophical

Society would be founded here at Christmas' (GA 260, 27 December 1923).

Thus when considered from an esoteric point of view, the General Anthroposophical Society was to become the representative of earthly humanity before the Time Spirit who now guides it, that is, before Michael himself. Hence after its founding Rudolf Steiner embarked with renewed energy upon unfolding to its members the mysteries of Michael, as the ruling Time Spirit and the inspirer of spiritual science. By this means a new path was indicated towards the common work of the Anthroposophical Society not only with Michael himself but also with the other Archai who in the higher worlds belong to his spiritual stream and who, as new group souls, wish to collaborate with humanity or with that part of it which yearns to present its spiritual interests before the ruling Time Spirit.[12]

8. The New Group Souls

Every anthroposophist who consistently studies the spiritual-scientific revelations of Rudolf Steiner will be struck all the more often by one of their distinctive qualities, namely, that particularly important fruits of his spiritual research were not infrequently mentioned by him only once and with extreme brevity. The impression arises that it was as though Rudolf Steiner was at such a moment awaiting a response from his listeners, in order that he might tell them more or add further details and correlations.

Such an inner position on the part of Rudolf Steiner was a direct consequence of his intimate connection with the Time Spirit, thus mirroring that quality of his which has been described above. Just as Michael himself in his rulership over humanity wholly reckons with man's individual freedom, so does the modern initiate, in working in the spirit of Michael, now depend upon the questions addressed to him. What for the first time manifested itself in the destiny of Parzival, who had to ask a question in the Grail castle, has in the Michael epoch become a basic feature of the new initiation founded upon the forces of the consciousness soul.

Among such results of Rudolf Steiner's spiritual-scientific research with a quite exceptional significance, but of which he spoke only very little, is his indication about *new group souls* contained in the lecture of 1 June 1908. There he speaks of how in the present time earthly human beings are awaited in the spiritual worlds by group souls, that is, hierarchic beings appointed for the leadership of various groups amongst mankind who, in contrast to previous group souls, wholly take into account human individuality and the attainment of freedom.

Rudolf Steiner described this quality, not shared by former group souls, in the following way: 'All the earlier group souls were beings who made people unfree. These new beings, however, are compatible with the total freedom, and the upholding, of human individuality' (GA 102, 1 June 1908). From this there follows something of extraordinary significance, namely, that with the appearance of such group souls in the world of the Hierarchies the spiritual foundation was laid for the first time in earthly evolution for a future free and conscious collaboration between human beings and the higher Hierarchies, the beginning of which was initiated in the present epoch of Michael's rulership over mankind.

It follows from what is imparted here by Rudolf Steiner that these new group souls in the spiritual worlds are in our time awaiting human beings who want to work together with them for the good of earthly evolution. While, however, fully acknowledging individual human freedom, they—as does Michael himself—*await* that moment when human beings themselves, out of their freedom and on the basis of a knowledge of the existence of these group souls as derived from anthroposophy, independently take up the resolve to work together with them. And this will become possible only if such people not only discover the knowledge about the new group souls, that is, the 'wisdom' about them as imparted by anthroposophy, but in their own midst achieve a true 'harmony of feelings'.

In the lecture referred to Rudolf Steiner describes both features of the new social forms of human beings in the following words: 'Those who will again grasp spiritual truth as it has been described will be led together of their own free will' (GA 102, 1 June 1908). Here the words 'spiritual truth' refer to the new esoteric wisdom that has been given to humanity today from the sources of spiritual science. And then Rudolf Steiner describes this second quality: 'Through individuals voluntarily allowing their feelings to stream together, something is formed which goes beyond the merely emancipated human being... The feelings streaming together in this way to a single focus once more give beings the opportunity of working as a kind of group soul, though in an altogether different sense from the former group souls' (ibid.). In these words the reference to the 'feelings' of human beings 'streaming to a single focus' speaks of the second quality of human social forms that is necessary for their collaboration with the new group souls.

In other words, the more intensely the feelings of those who are working spiritually can unite in one common focus, whose earthly context is to be *shared* esoteric work, and after the Christmas Conference 'the soul of the Anthroposophical Society, namely the School of Spiritual Science at the Goetheanum' (GA 260, 28 December

1923), so much the more will exalted group souls be able to unite with such spiritual work.

It is not difficult to see from this that the main condition for such a collaboration with the new group souls is that human individuals working together develop two basic qualities which have always been characteristic of any true human initiate. For this reason Rudolf Steiner calls them the *Masters of Wisdom and of the Harmony of Feelings*. But what in the past could be attained only by individual high initiates, from the moment of the new group souls' emergence into earthly evolution—whose activity coincides where humanity is concerned with the beginning of the modern Michael epoch—this must now extend to all human beings. For through anthroposophy, anyone can now—albeit to an initial degree—attain both qualities, the individual and the social. By his own efforts he must first form a relationship with the new spiritual *wisdom* proclaimed by anthroposophy by means of thinking, and then add to this the capacity to unite with other spiritually striving human beings in a new social community, whose task is collaborating with hierarchic spirits on the basis of the *harmony of feelings* achieved by its members and the mutual acknowledgement of the full autonomy of the human individual and his spiritual freedom. In this way such groups will embark upon the path of the true *Masters* of modern initiation, which in our time is an initiation of the will.[13] In time they will be able truly to approach that ideal of social life and activity represented by the highest association of the spiritual teachers of humanity. In accordance with esoteric tradition, Rudolf Steiner calls it the 'Great White Lodge of the Rulership of Mankind'; and it derives inspirations from the sources of the Time Spirit.

Moreover, mentioning in this context the 'Theosophical Society' as 'a first example ... of such a voluntary group' testifies to how Rudolf Steiner from the very beginning of his spiritual activity, while he was still General Secretary of the German Section of the Theosophical Society (from 1902), endeavoured to establish such forms of common work of its members as enabled people to learn to collaborate with the new group souls. 'The attempt had to be made to create a group in which people find themselves together without the differentiation of the old group soul's nature, and there will be many such associations in the future' (ibid.). The General Anthroposophical Society founded at the Christmas Conference is a prime example of such a social form, wholly orientated as it is towards a common spiritual task together with the new group souls.

Here, however, a decisive question arises. If the former group souls of mankind have led humanity without knowing anything about the mystery of human freedom and, hence, have not taken it into account in the way they have fulfilled their task, whence have the new group souls—to put it in human language—'learnt' this new capacity? Who told them about it in the supersensible worlds?

In order to answer this question, it is necessary above all to turn one's attention to the fact that Rudolf Steiner makes a definite distinction between earthly or human freedom and freedom of a cosmic nature. This second concept of freedom is very difficult, and perhaps for this reason Rudolf Steiner himself did not characterise it anywhere in detail. In the present context the most important indication about it is contained in an article that he wrote already after the Christmas Conference and entitled 'Michael's Mission in the Cosmic Age of Human Freedom'. There Rudolf Steiner first very briefly touches upon the concept of freedom that he presented in *The Philosophy of Freedom*, and then compares it with the concept of 'cosmic freedom', knowledge of which can be acquired only in the sphere of Michael. 'When the work of Michael at the present time is approached through spiritual experience, it becomes possible, from the spiritual-scientific point of view, to obtain light on the cosmic nature of *freedom*' (GA 26, article cited above; the italics are Rudolf Steiner's).

Later in the same article Rudolf Steiner speaks of a 'spiritual companionship with Michael' leading to such an experience of 'the cosmic nature of freedom'. Rudolf Steiner described this 'companionship with Michael' at greater length in the karma lectures. In the spiritual worlds it leads to his supersensible School, where he himself appears not only as the representative of Sun wisdom but as the great Teacher of cosmic freedom. For in our time Michael indicates to man with his newly acquired freedom the modern path to Christ, who then gives him the possibility of uniting with his spiritual or cosmic origins and thereby finding a path into the future.

Precisely because Michael is in the higher worlds the great teacher of cosmic freedom, the path whereby human freedom is made a reality on Earth in the sense of *The Philosophy of Freedom* leads to a spiritual encounter with him in the higher worlds. '*When man seeks freedom* without inclining towards egoism, when freedom becomes for him pure love for the action which is to be performed [in the sense of the second part of *The Philosophy of Freedom*], then it is possible for him to approach Michael' (GA 26, 'The World-Thoughts in the Working of Michael and in the Working of Ahriman'; italics are Rudolf Steiner's).

Rudolf Steiner wrote his *Philosophy of Freedom* from such a proximity to Michael. For as he himself said, in the period when he was working on this book in Weimar he was himself for the first time granted a spiritual meeting with Michael in the supersensible world nearest to the earthly world.[14]

Thus the knowledge of the 'cosmic nature of freedom' in proximity to Michael and at the same time the experiencing of it in the earthly world, as came fully to expression in the book *The Philosophy of Freedom*, were for Rudolf Steiner two mutually inseparable processes which laid the foundation for the ensuing development of anthroposophy. This sheds light on one very important aspect of the teaching in the supersensible Michael School. This was, alongside much else, also *an instruction in cosmic freedom*, at the centre of which stood Michael himself as the 'spiritual hero of freedom'.

In this connection it is striking that the metamorphosis of the old mysteries into the new mysteries, which took place in the supersensible Michael School, was at the same time accompanied by the elevation of their wisdom from the sentient soul and the intellectual or mind soul—where it had been experienced by their earthly participants during the third and fourth post-Atlantean epochs—to the consciousness soul. This meant that at the time when this epoch had just begun on Earth (1413), in the high Sun sphere a group of human souls who were between death and a new birth received a teaching regarding the essence of the old mysteries from the standpoint of the consciousness soul, that is, in the completely new form in which the principle of heavenly anthroposophy and of its focus, the new Christian mysteries, was founded. 'In the heights, in the spiritual world, there was this sublime School, gathering together the old initiate-wisdom *in a new form*, calling up into the intelligence-filled consciousness, *into the consciousness soul* of predestined human beings between death and rebirth, what in earlier times had been man's treasury of wisdom in the intellectual or mind soul, the sentient soul and so forth' (GA 240, 20 July 1924).

The mentioning in this connection of the intellectual or mind soul and the sentient soul is indicative of the mysteries deriving from the fourth and third post-Atlantean epochs (the Graeco-Roman and Ancient Egyptian), when these two soul members were being developed amongst the whole of humanity, while the phrase 'and so forth' refers to the mysteries of the second (Ancient Persian) and the first (Ancient Indian) post-Atlantean epochs, when these two bodies were being developed. Of no less importance here are the words 'in a new way', testifying as they do to how in the Michael School the ancient wisdom of the mysteries was renewed out of the forces of the Mystery of Golgotha. For as was said above, in the Michael School it was a question of founding a new cosmic Christianity.[15]

In characterising the Michael School, Rudolf Steiner spoke on several occasions of how its content was perceived not only by human souls but equally by hierarchic beings who were also participating in it, that is, beings who—in contrast to human beings—have never incarnated on Earth. Thus Michael's words, transmitted by Rudolf Steiner as follows, were addressed not only to human souls but also to these hierarchic beings: 'Let us bring it [the content of the old mysteries] to the consciousness of those spiritual beings who are around me, those beings who never appear in earthly bodies but have their existence only in an etheric form. But let us bring it, too, to those souls who have often lived on Earth in physical bodies, those who are actually there now, and who belong to the Michael community—let us bring it to the consciousness of these human souls. We will image forth *the great initiation-teaching* which once streamed down in the ancient fashion, through the mysteries, to the Earth. We will present this to the souls of those who in their life of intelligence were linked with Michael' (GA 240, 20 July 1924).

Here, too, the words about the 'great initiation-teaching' relate not to the content of the old mysteries, for he goes on to say that they existed on Earth 'once in the ancient fashion', but to the new mysteries, whose source goes back to the Deed of Christ on Golgotha.

If we now recall that, in the Michael School, among the beings who had never incarnated on Earth and received his teaching there were not only numerous elemental spirits but also a whole series of beings of all three categories of the Third Hierarchy—that is, all the Angels, Archangels and even Archai (see the quotation above) connected with the supersensible stream of Michael, we may then find an answer to the question as to whence the new group souls acquired knowledge of cosmic and human freedom. For purely by learning this in the supersensible Michael School, they were then able to embark upon an entirely new form of leadership of earthly human beings, in full compatibility with their individual freedom: the Angels—leadership of individual groups; the Archangels—large associations; and the Archai—human social forms aspiring to represent the whole of humanity.

The fact that by the 'new group souls' Rudolf Steiner in the lecture cited means beings of the Third Hierarchy follows from the 'connections of an aesthetic, moral and intellectual character' mentioned in it which, in the process of transition from the earlier 'group soul nature to the free group associations' (GA 102, 1 June 1908), that is from working with the old group souls to working with the new, must from our time onwards gradually replace all racial, national and blood (family) ties.

On more than one occasion Rudolf Steiner mentions these three injunctions in a somewhat modified sequence, as having their spiritual origins corresponding to the stages of the astral plane, Lower and Higher Devachan (see GA 130, 4 November 1911).

Intellectual impulses (wisdom)—astral plane
Aesthetic impulses (beauty) —Lower Devachan
Moral impulses (goodness) —Higher Devachan

In the individual life of a human being the capacity for experiencing these three impulses, which also correspond to truth, beauty and goodness in the Rosicrucian tradition, is incorporated in the process of his acquiring the skills of learning to walk, speech and thinking in the first three years of earthly life (before the awakening of individual ego-consciousness).[16] Thus the Archai bring to man's being the forces of uprightness of posture and at the same time the capacity to take hold of moral impulses from Higher Devachan; the Archangels bring the power of speech and the capacity to perceive beauty from Lower Devachan, and the Angels the faculty of thinking (knowledge) from the astral plane. Through this the first-named incorporate amongst mankind forces leading to the ultimate transformation within it of all racial differences, the second work similarly with national differences and the third with those of family ancestry.

In mentioning in what he says about the new group souls these three impulses of the moral, the aesthetic and the intellectual, Rudolf Steiner is indirectly referring to the beings of the Third Hierarchy standing behind them, collaboration with whom serves to strengthen within human beings the forces of truth, beauty and goodness and, in a social context, those of freedom, equality and brotherhood such as lead to the establishing on Earth of a social threefoldness, the only social order which corresponds to the step of a conscious partnership between the Gods and human beings also in the social sphere.[17]

Such a new collaboration between the Gods and human beings will, however, be possible only in the event that human beings themselves reach towards the Gods and consciously take hold of the 'spiritual hands' that are extended to them; in other words, if on Earth there are enough people prepared for this by anthroposophy and wanting to collaborate with the Hierarchies not only individually but also as a new human association. For 'it will lie in the souls of human beings themselves whether or not they give as many as possible of such higher souls the opportunity of descending to man'. And 'the more that associations are formed where feelings of fellowship are developed with complete freedom, the more exalted beings will descend' (GA 102, 1 June 1908).

This means that if 'feelings of fellowship' are developed by anthroposophists on the level of the various groups and branches, Angels who have passed through the Michael School will be able to unite with them in the capacity of new group souls. (As we have already seen, Rudolf Steiner referred to them when characterising the nature of the 'reversed cultus' in anthroposophical groups or branches.) Then if a similar feeling of community spreads among anthroposophists on the level of national Societies, Archangels who have passed through the Michael School will be able to unite with such groups; and if a community-consciousness between anthroposophists permeates the entire General Anthroposophical Society founded at the Christmas Conference, the Archai who have passed through the Michael School will be able to unite with their spiritual work.

And on the other hand, 'the more that people are divided, the fewer exalted [group] souls will descend into the human sphere' (ibid.). In other words, if disagreements in the Anthroposophical Society take hold of its individual groups, the Angels connected with them will fall away; if they spread to national Societies, Archangels will withdraw from them; and if such a destiny were to befall the General Anthroposophical Society (as was the case in the conflicts in the 1930s and 1940s) the Archai who passed through the supersensible School would also abandon it, as would the ruling Time Spirit who leads the entire Michael stream in the higher worlds.

As with everything in the world, however, for something of this kind to happen as part of the process is not in itself fatal. Hence a weakened or a well-nigh forfeited connection with the Hierarchies can—especially in the epoch of freedom—be restored anew, if only people can be found on Earth who are capable of filling themselves with enthusiasm for having a relationship to such an ideal and beginning working together upon its realisation.

Only in a more distant future—if earthly humanity finally misses such an opportunity or actually rejects it—would something irredeemable take place. Thus in the lecture referred to Rudolf Steiner felt duty-bound to indicate what would happen if people (and in his lecture he was in the first instance addressing anthroposophists) were unable to come to a single wisdom[18] and a harmony of their feelings, in order on this basis to begin working together with the new group souls (spirits of the Third Hierarchy). For then in the course of further evolution the human soul that has emancipated itself from the spiritual world, having missed the opportunity consciously to form an attachment to the hierarchic cosmos, will become 'itself a kind of elemental being' (ibid.). And these elemental beings who would thus emerge from human beings 'would be of quite an evil nature' (ibid).

Whereas if human beings avail themselves of this unique possibility presented to them today in the Anthroposophical Society, if out of their own freedom and spiritual knowledge they themselves find the path to a social collaboration with the Gods, the whole of earthly evolution will take a direction leading to the attainment of its principal purpose, which Rudolf Steiner formulated in the cited lecture as follows: 'The more exalted beings will descend to human beings, the more rapidly the earthly planet will be spiritualised' (ibid.).

On closer study of Rudolf Steiner's spiritual-scientific indications regarding the conditions necessary for the collaboration of human beings with the new group souls, it is possible to discern in them three successive stages:

Knowledge of the spiritual truths of anthroposophy in *thinking*;
Free streaming together of *feelings* around a single focus;
Attaining of social unity in the *will*.

Of the three conditions the main one is the second, which can be attained by human beings only by dint of their developing *heart-thinking*. For just as in the human organism the heart is its living centre, so in every true human community a kind of single focus, or 'social heart', needs to arise whither all the best and most spiritual feelings of the community can stream as to an invisible 'focal point'.

In one of the esoteric lessons Rudolf Steiner refers to how the flow of blood to the heart with a feeling of fear, and its flow away from it to the periphery with a feeling of shame, are, respectively, conditions anticipating the future Jupiter and reminiscent of Old Moon. (See GA 245, 16 January 1908.) From this it follows that in a social respect the movement of the feelings of members of a community to the periphery, leading to dissociation and conflict, testify to the preponderance within it of forces of the past, of forces of old, Moon karma, whereas the movement of the feelings of its members to a single focus or centre, strengthening its unity and furthering collaboration with the new group souls, represents an anticipation of the condition of the future Jupiter (sixth cultural epoch).

In the esoteric lesson referred to Rudolf Steiner describes this future Jupiter condition in the following words: 'When the time has come where Jupiter consciousness dawns, and man enters once more into a harmonious relationship with the forces of the cosmos, he will bring his self-conscious sense of his own identity to the safety of the new state of consciousness, so that man will then be an independent ego and nevertheless in harmony with the universe' (ibid.). In these words it is sufficient to replace the words 'cosmos' and 'universe' with 'social environment', that is, make the transition from the plane of the future Jupiter to that of the sixth cultural epoch, which anticipates it in the social sphere, and we have precisely that condition which Rudolf Steiner described as the necessary condition for the combined activity of human beings and the new group souls from amongst the beings of the Third Hierarchy.

This is further confirmed in that, on the future Jupiter—having attained the stage of Angel—man will be fully integrated into the circle of the Third Hierarchy, on Venus—on attaining the stage of Archangel—into the sphere of the Second Hierarchy and on Vulcan—on attaining the stage of Archai—into the sphere of the First Hierarchy.

As we have seen, bringing about in a group that social condition where a free collaboration with the new group souls is possible entails the development of *heart-thinking* on the social plane. Michael wishes in our time to lead mankind to this heart-thinking: 'He liberates thought from the sphere of the head; he clears the way for it to the heart' (GA 26, *Anthroposophical Leading Thoughts*). Thus he impels human beings to an experience of a new enthusiasm, the ultimate source of which is the 'heavenly thunderstorm' (described at the beginning of this extended essay), representing the very first stage of the heavenly preparation of anthroposophy. 'He enkindles enthusiasm in the feelings, so that the human mind can be filled with devotion for all that can be experienced in the *light of thought*. The age of Michael has dawned. Hearts are beginning to have thoughts; spiritual fervour is now proceeding not merely from mystical obscurity but from a thought-imbued clarity of soul' (ibid.; the italics are Rudolf Steiner's). But the foundation for this 'thought-imbued clarity of soul' whence a true Michaelic enthusiasm must now spring was established in that combined cosmic deed of the Hierarchies, through which the 'man of the heart' became the 'man of the head', thereby acquiring for the first time the possibility of experiencing his thoughts in a state of complete clarity of soul.

This also has a very direct connection with the forming of the anthroposophical community in the spirit of the Christmas Conference. Thus in the same article Rudolf Steiner wrote directly addressing the karma of anthroposophists who have, by virtue of their relationship with Michael in past lives, passed through his supersensible School: 'When those who in their former earthly life received their thoughts by inspiration, i.e. were servants of Michael, had returned to earthly life at the close of the 19th century, they felt *urged towards a voluntary Michael community* of this description' (ibid.). The word 'urged' in the present instance in no way implies any contradiction with the freedom of the individual; it merely signifies that the foundation and at the same time the spiritual source of such a *free* forming on Earth of the new Michaelic community (the Anthroposophical Society) is the common Sun karma of all anthroposophists, which has been formed through their passing together through the teaching in the Michael School together with beings of the Third Hierarchy.

Thus Michael's endeavour now is that, through the collaboration of human beings with one another and at the same time with the Hierarchies who serve him, the spiritual impulses of his supersensible School may work on Earth also *on the social plane*. The foundation for this was laid at the Christmas Conference through the threefold structure of the Anthroposophical Society described in the previous chapter, the threefold form of the Foundation Stone and its Meditation.

In order to understand this one needs to bear in mind that, within the Third Hierarchy, the Angels represent its impulses as a whole, that is, the forces of the Holy Spirit working through it; the Archangels represent in its entirety the Second Hierarchy, behind which stand the forces of the Son; and the Archai represent the First Hierarchy, through whom the Father forces are active. From this follows the participation of the Third Hierarchy not only in the coming into being of the Foundation Stone Meditation but also in the creation of the supersensible Foundation Stone, in which the forces of the Holy Trinity were working together with the beings of the Third Hierarchy. For within the Third Hierarchy the Archai are connected with the Father God, the Archangels with the Son and the Angels with the Holy Spirit.[19]

Thus one can say that the relationship with the Third Hierarchy, especially with those of its representatives who passed through the Sun School of Michael, permeated the entire Christmas Conference. And the General Anthroposophical Society was in an esoteric sense created in order that human beings might learn to work with the Gods.

9. The Grail Mystery and the Third Hierarchy

Rudolf Steiner's mentioning of the participation of a whole rank of Angels, Archangels and Archai in the Michael School poses the question as to the karmic sources of their affinity with the Michael stream and his supersensible School. If one bears in mind that in this School the foundation of a new, cosmic Christianity was laid, and that at the same time it initiated the heavenly preparation of anthroposophy, which Rudolf Steiner called a modern 'Grail science', thereby connecting it with this central stream of esoteric Christianity, we shall have what we need to answer the question that has been raised.

For in establishing spiritual science on the Earth as a modern Grail science, Rudolf Steiner was consciously forming a link with that stream of esoteric Christianity which has for centuries borne this name.[20] It follows from this that the heavenly preparation of anthroposophy, which is associated with the renewal of Christianity in the Michael School, was also connected with the continuation of the Grail mysteries, though not on Earth but in the spiritual world.

The Grail mysteries have on two previous occasions abided in the higher worlds: in the period between the life at the Turning Point of Time of Joseph of Arimathea and Titurel in the 8th century, who built the first Grail castle in Northern Spain and initiated its esoteric stream on the Earth. For a second time the Grail was taken back to the spiritual world in the 9th century at the end of the time of Parzival, where it was entrusted to spiritual beings of the higher Hierarchies right until the founding on Earth of anthroposophy, as a modern Grail science. Until this time 'spiritual beings protected the world-pictures in which the secrets of Golgotha were living' (GA 26, 'Gnosis and Anthroposophy') and which reflected the substance of the Holy Grail.

Only upon this foundation in the Michael School could a new, *cosmic Christianity* be founded, whose pictorial content was then for the first time elevated to the consciousness soul of the human beings taking part in it. We can understand the significance of this if we bear in mind that the consciousness soul is in future to be transformed by man into the imaginative soul (GA 145, 29 March 1913), which will then bear within itself new clairvoyant powers capable of apprehending in full consciousness objective imaginations from the spiritual world.

But what was formerly to arise on earth from the free endeavours of man can be experienced by him prophetically in the spiritual world before birth. From this it follows that the elevation to the consciousness soul (in the spiritual worlds it is already possessed of clairvoyance and, hence, works as the imaginative soul) of the content of the new mysteries in the Michael School was inseparably connected with the receiving into it of the 'world-pictures' that bear within themselves the secret of the Mystery of Golgotha, that is, the content of the Grail chalice.

For as we have seen, the metamorphosis of the old mysteries into the new was brought about by Michael on the foundation of spiritual forces which entered into earthly evolution as the result of the Mystery of Golgotha, a kind of 'extract' of which was from the outset kept in the Grail chalice, whence follows that the spiritual content of the holy chalice played a central part also in the Michael School.

Precisely through their imaginative character, the 'world-pictures' of the Grail played a particular role in the subsequent supersensible cultus—the concluding stage of the heavenly preparation of anthroposophy, as a modern Grail science.

From this it follows that those beings who were the guardians of the Grail at the time when it was taken from the Earth and abided in the spiritual worlds were those who from the outset had belonged to the supersensible stream of Michael, and then participated in his School. Hence Rudolf Steiner was able to write that 'in our age—out of the consciousness soul and in the light of Michael's activity—a new and full understanding of the Mystery of Golgotha needs to develop', and that 'anthroposophy strives for this new understanding' (GA 26, 'Gnosis and Anthroposophy'). And it strives for it because the foundation for this was laid already in the process of its supersensible preparation in the spiritual world.

For if the 'great initiation-teaching' (GA 240, 20 July 1924), then called by Rudolf Steiner the 'science of the Grail' (to which, according to him, the anthroposophical path of initiation described in *Occult*

Science leads), was established in the Michael School, it follows from this that in the Michael School itself there was to exist a direct relationship between it and the Grail mysteries in the spiritual world. Such a relationship, however, could be brought about only by the actual spiritual (hierarchic) beings who had from the outset been associated with the supersensible mysteries of the holy chalice and then participated in the Michael School under his leadership.

Rudolf Steiner refers to this in the following words: 'A Michael host gathered together in supersensible regions, receiving in the spiritual world the teachings which had been imparted by the Michael teachers from the old Alexander time, *the Michael teachers from the time of the Grail tradition*, those Michael teachers whose presence can be felt in impulses such as that of Arthur's Round Table' (GA 240, 21 August 1924).

In other words, in the Michael School there was formed a community of a unique kind, consisting of formerly incarnated human souls, elemental spirits and beings of the Third Hierarchy, who have together taken in the 'teachings of the Michael teachers' from the pre-Christian mysteries through to the time of Alexander the Great, when with the burning of the Temple of Ephesus they began to leave the Earth; then from the time of the mysteries of the knights of King Arthur, whose task was to bring about the transition from the pre-Christian mysteries to the Christian mysteries; and finally, from the mystery-stream of the Holy Grail, which for several centuries has been the principal stream of esoteric Christianity. Moreover, what is especially pertinent in the passage quoted is the reference to that transitional period when there existed on the Earth not the Grail mysteries as such but only their 'tradition' (12th–13th centuries), that is to say, when the Grail itself was taken from the Earth and preserved in the spiritual world by those hierarchic spirits who were at the time participating in the Michael School, thereby forming a living succession between it and the mysteries of the Holy Grail. As a result of this the heavenly anthroposophy was prepared in the supersensible worlds in such a way that it could become on Earth not only a 'science of the spirit' but also a 'science of the Grail'.

That the spirits of all three categories of the Third Hierarchy, in particular, were amongst the supersensible guardians of the Grail in the higher worlds is borne out by that mighty imagination which Rudolf

Steiner laid at the foundation of the whole of Waldorf Education. At the beginning of his main pedagogical course of lectures, bearing the title 'A General Study of Man as a Basis for Education' (GA 293), he gave the first Waldorf teachers an imagination of a supersensible chalice, representing the essential aspect of the modern Grail mysteries, one that is associated with the possibility of a combined activity on the part of the Gods and human beings in our time.

It is merely necessary meditatively to immerse oneself in this imagination, and to experience in it the forming of an inner spiritual space (an aura of strength) from the forces of the Angels, the coming into being of the imagination of a chalice from the activity of the Archangels and its being filled with spiritual substance from the essential nature of the Archai, for the modern mysteries of the Holy Grail to appear before us in all their supersensible reality and world significance.

But the spirits of the Third Hierarchy also participated in a similar way in the forming of the Foundation Stone of the Christmas Conference. Only now, inasmuch as the event in question was not simply a meditative experience of the reality of the Grail but a free creative act wrought by Rudolf Steiner out of the forces which entered into earthly evolution through the Mystery of Golgotha, the separate stages are in reverse order. For in the one case one is speaking of a shared meditative experience of a higher reality, while in the other of its creation. Thus the Foundation Stone was created by Rudolf Steiner out of the substance of the Archai, its imaginative form out of the forces of the Archangels, and the thought-aura surrounding it out of the forces of the angels, through which were working the forces of the Holy Trinity, as was described above.[21]

Nevertheless, in both cases they were those same Angels, Archangels and Archai who were first the guardians of the Grail in the supersensible worlds and then passed through the supersensible Michael School, in order to become from our time onwards the new group souls of mankind, with a knowledge of the secret of cosmic and human freedom.

10. The Tasks of the Anthroposophical Society

Rudolf Steiner's words, quoted above, to the effect that the work of human beings with the new group souls will lead to the gradual spiritualisation of the entire earthly planet are almost an exact repetition of that passage at the end of *Occult Science* where he writes of how the aim of earthly evolution can be achieved by human beings only through the Mystery of Golgotha. That is why this aim or 'higher ideal' is revealed to man out of a modern 'Grail knowledge', as the focus of the new Christian mysteries.

In *Occult Science* Rudolf Steiner formulates this ideal in the following words: 'We see then that the "knowledge of the Grail" culminates in the highest imaginable ideal of human evolution—the ideal of spiritualisation, brought about by man's own efforts' (GA 13, ch. 6). And then Rudolf Steiner continues: 'This spiritualisation is the ultimate outcome of the harmony achieved in the fifth and sixth epochs of the present age—the harmony between the powers of reason and feeling man has by now acquired, and the true knowledge of the spiritual world' (ibid.). From these words it follows that, from our time onwards, it will become a matter of achieving an inner harmony between the powers of reason and feeling and supersensible knowledge, that is, between the powers of the sentient soul and the intellectual soul, on the one hand, and, on the other, of the consciousness soul, which—on being elevated to the stage of imaginative soul—achieves knowledge of the spiritual world out of its own forces.

The foundation for such a harmony, as we saw above, was laid by Michael in his supersensible School in the souls of those human beings who, by virtue of their karma, were honoured with participating in it, in order then on Earth to become anthroposophists. By raising the content of the ancient mysteries from the sentient soul and intellectual soul to the consciousness soul (of course in its most spiritualised condition, inasmuch as one is speaking about processes in the high Sun sphere), Michael was thereby implanting in the souls of future anthroposophists the yearning for the 'highest imaginable ideal of human evolution', which is what has led these souls to anthroposophy.

It also follows from these words that the foundation for this development is to be laid amongst mankind during the present fifth and the ensuing sixth cultural epochs, at the threshold between which the problem of the higher synthesis between the individual and the social aspirations of humanity must finally be resolved—which is possible only as a result of bringing the karma between human individuals into order. It was also for the fulfilment of this task, in a manner befitting the Time Spirit, that Rudolf Steiner, as we have seen, gave the founding impulses at the Christmas Conference and especially after it in the karma lectures, inasmuch as its fulfilment forms an essential part of the new Christian mysteries.

Two kinds of faculties need to be developed by mankind for this aim. Over the course of the remaining part of the fifth post-Atlantean epoch there must be achieved within humanity the capacity of forming a pictorial experience of another person, leading to perceiving the eternal aura of his inner being. (See GA 185, 26 October 1918.) For without such an imaginative perception, the task of bringing karma between human individuals into order will not be brought to a conclusion. The second problem, the resolution of which will occupy not only the remaining part of the fifth post-Atlantean epoch but also a significant part of the sixth, will consist in the necessity of entering into a conscious connection with the beings of the Third Hierarchy, the Angels, Archangels and Archai' (ibid.). And in order that the connection with them might be developed with due regard for human freedom, it is necessary to embark upon the fulfilment of this task together with those same spirits of all three categories of the Third Hierarchy who had previously themselves been prepared for such work in the supersensible Michael School.

In this sense the very thought that in the Sun School of Michael a group of human souls under his direct guidance has passed through a 'training course' *together* with chosen spirits of all three categories of beings of the Third Hierarchy is capable of filling the heart of every anthroposophist with a genuine enthusiasm and a real spiritual joy.

For the knowledge that a whole rank of Angels, Archangels and even Archai is awaiting free collaboration with human beings in the spiritual world, a rank of beings who—like us—are deeply connected with the heavenly stream of Michael and are, therefore, not alien or unfamiliar beings to us but are those spirits of the higher Hierarchies with whom a heavenly, Michaelic karma has long connected us, can imbue us with those spiritual forces of which we are in need if we are to be able in freedom to continue the forming of this karma already on Earth and thereby make the intended esoteric aim of the Anthroposophical Society a reality. One thing only is necessary for the fulfilment of this aim: we must *remember* our spiritual tasks of which we became aware in the Michael School when we contemplated the all-encompassing cosmic thunderstorm called forth by the higher Hierarchies for the transformation of man's being, and then became immersed in the depths of our will in the cosmic imaginative cultus.

In other words, only an inner relationship of anthroposophists with their Sun, Michaelic karma can enable them to become worthy representatives of the new mysteries founded by Rudolf Steiner at the Christmas Conference.

After the two stages that have been described, leading earthly evolution to its ultimate goal of the spiritualisation of the Earth—after the conscious work of human beings on their karma and the collaboration with beings of the Third Hierarchy—a third stage will follow in the future. It will consist in a process of gradually liberating the kingdoms of nature, a process which will begin in the sixth cultural epoch and will continue throughout the seventh. However, it will conclude only in the great sixth period which follows it. The following words of Paul the Apostle to the Romans prophetically refer to this distant future: 'For we know that the whole creation has been groaning in travail together until now', and so '[it] waits with eager longing for the revealing of the Sons of God ... in hope [that] the creation itself will be set free from its bondage to decay and obtain the glorious liberty of the children of God' (Romans 8:22, 19–21).

In this way all the kingdoms of nature, which had formerly descended to a stage lower than the human stage in order that man might raise himself up and reach the goal of his evolution, will in the distant future also, through his conscious collaboration with the spirits of the Third Hierarchy, be received into the sphere of human freedom. In modern initiation the Great Guardian of the Threshold refers man to this stage: 'Hitherto you have only realised yourself, but now, having yourself become free, you can liberate all your companions in the sense-world. Until today you have striven as an individual; now make yourself a member of the whole, so that you may bring into the supersensible world not yourself alone, but everything else that exists in the world of the senses' (GA 10, 'Life and Death. The Great Guardian of the Threshold'). In this process those elemental spirits, who together with human beings and selected beings of the Third Hierarchy have passed through the training in the Michael School, will also have a special part to play.

Thus after the beginning of the combined activity of the Gods and human beings, that is, through the gradual receiving of the latter into the condition of being 'the sons of God', which is to say, into the totality of the hierarchic whole of our cosmos, there ensues the redemption by human beings of all creation.

The entire process that has been described concludes with a final, fourth stage, when the spiritualisation of the whole Earth will be achieved. This will take place at the very end of the present earthly aeon. The Christ Himself, as the new Spirit of the Earth and the Leader of its entire evolution, will play a central part in this process.

The four stages that have been surveyed can be summarised in the following way:

1. The work of human beings on their common (new) karma.
2. The collaboration with beings of the Third Hierarchy (the new group souls).
3. The redemption by man of the kingdoms of nature.
4. The spiritualisation of the Earth at the end of the earthly aeon.

All this finds its correspondence in the content of the Foundation Stone Meditation. For this purpose it is necessary merely to take its four parts in succession but in a reverse order. Then its concluding, fourth part will be indicative of the work of human beings together on their karma in the spirit of Christ as its new Lord.

That good may become
What we from our hearts would found
What we from our heads would direct
In conscious
Willing.

The line 'That good may become, what we ...', understood in the light of the reference to the working of the 'Christ-Sun' that precedes it, signifies that *combined* work of human beings in the realm of karma, the fruits of which can increase the forces of goodness in the whole of earthly evolution.

Then in the third part of the Foundation Stone Meditation it speaks of the conscious union of man, once he has attained the stage of freedom in his ego, with the 'world light' of the 'aims of Gods' sent down to human beings by members of the Third Hierarchy as goals relating to man's individual development (Angels), the evolution of nations (Archangels) and the evolution of the whole of humanity (Archai).

Where the eternal aims of Gods
World-Being's Light
On thine own I
Bestow
For thy free willing.

Such a conscious and free collaboration with the beings of the Third Hierarchy corresponds to the second stage of the development that is being described.

Then in the second part of the Meditation, through the union of man's ego with the 'deeds of the world's becoming', in which the 'World-I' of Christ has lived since the Mystery of Golgotha, the redemption of the whole natural environment can be achieved, gazing with hope upon man's achievement of the stage of free 'sonship of God', in order to become its redeemer.

Where the surging deeds
Of the world's becoming
Thine own I [of man]
Unite
With the World-I.

Finally, in the third part of the Meditation there is an indication of how, as a result of the conscious ascent of man's individual ego—imbued with the Christ impulse—into the sphere of the highest existence of 'world-creating', it will be able in future, 'through its own work', to spiritualise the entire earthly planet.

In the process of the spiritualising of nature, not only man but also spirits of the Second and—with the eventual spiritualising of the Earth—spirits of the First Hierarchy will participate, collaboration with whom will then come about through the mediation of beings of the Third Hierarchy, as described above.

Where in the wielding will
Of world-creating
Thine own I
Comes to being
Within God's I.

The point of departure for the whole path of development that has been described is the work of human beings on the transformation of their own karma. For once having begun this work, they will have laid the foundation for the entire future evolution of the Earth, which is to say, for the three subsequent stages of its spiritualisation. Thus through receiving into his ego the 'world-light' of the 'eternal aims' of the Third Hierarchy, man will become the conscious collaborator of the Gods; through uniting his ego with the 'World-I' of Christ, he will discover the forces for redeeming the kingdoms of nature that surround him; and through permeating his ego with the forces of 'God's I', the world Creator, he will embark upon spiritualising the entire earthly planet. And throughout this path, working together with him, he will be helped by beings of the Third Hierarchy; by the Angels in comprehending the 'aims of Gods' and receiving into themselves their 'world light'; by the Archangels in the transformation of the kingdoms of nature; and by the Archai in the spiritualising of the Earth.

Thus only through working with the Hierarchies, beginning with the nearest, the Third, and, amongst them, especially with those spirits who have together with human beings passed through the teaching in the School of Michael will the possibility gradually open up for man to embark upon the process of universal spiritualisation, that is, upon imbuing not only himself but also nature (creation) and the entire Earth with the forces of the Spirit who entered into earthly evolution through Christ's Resurrection in the Mystery of Golgotha.

'May human beings hear it!'—with this call the elemental spirits who passed through the Sun School of Michael address themselves today to human beings. They summon man with the help of modern spiritual science to awaken in the sphere of the world thoughts of the Spirit, that is, in the sphere of Michael, as the Spirit of our time, which is to say the leading representative of the impulse of the Holy Spirit amongst mankind. For on this new and free relationship with the Spirit of our time and the beings of the Third Hierarchy who serve him depends not only the earthly destiny of the General Anthroposophical Society, but the entire future of mankind.

In the world-thoughts of the Spirit the soul awakens.
Per Spiritum Sanctum reviviscimus.

Notes

1. Regarding Rudolf Steiner's uniting himself even to the extent of his own karma with the Anthroposophical Society at its founding at the Christmas Conference, see further in S.O. Prokofieff, *May Human Beings Hear It! The Mystery of the Christmas Conference*, Sussex 2004, ch. 8, 'Rudolf Steiner and the Karma of the Anthroposophical Society'.
2. That only the First Hierarchy works in the universe right down into physical matter, Rudolf Steiner confirms as follows: 'The First and strongest Hierarchy reveals itself as the spiritually active principle within the physical. It makes the physical world into a cosmos. The Third and Second Hierarchy are the beings who minister to it in this activity' (GA 26, Leading Thought 71).
3. There is much to be said for the suggestion that the elemental spirits that passed through the teaching in the Sun School of Michael are those who in the Foundation Stone Meditation call on anthroposophists to recall their presence together in the supersensible School: 'May human beings hear it!'
4. See Rudolf Steiner, *Occult Science*, the chapter on initiation (GA 13).
5. What is being referred to here is a *different* stream of the Cosmic Intelligence from that which entered human souls from the Sun sphere of Michael approximately from the 9th century AD. (See GA 240, 19 July 1924.)
6. According to Rudolf Steiner's spiritual-scientific research, man's ego (and his astral body) always leave the physical and etheric bodies through the head, and in the morning enter them by way of the limbs. (See GA 239, 14 June 1924.)
7. See W.J. Stein, 'The Hague Conversation', published in W.J. Stein/Rudolf Steiner, *Dokumentation eines wegweisenden Zusammenwirkens*, Dornach 1985.
8. Only once in an evening lecture did Rudolf Steiner fleetingly mention that in the last third of the 19th century the modern Michael age began. (See GA 233, 29 December 1923.)
9. See further regarding this process in S.O. Prokofieff, *May Human Beings Hear It! The Mysteries of the Christmas Conference*, ch. 2, 'The Mystery Act of the Foundation Stone Laying on 25 December 1923'.
10. Ernst Lehrs, *Gelebte Erwartung*, Stuttgart 1979, p. 321.
11. See further in S.O. Prokofieff, *May Human Beings Hear It! The Mystery of the Christmas Conference*, Ch. 8.

12. Of course, not all Archai are Time Spirits, just as not all Archangels are leaders of nations and not all Angels are Guardian Angels of individual human beings. One also needs to bear in mind that in the spiritual worlds there are hierarchic beings who in their development are in the process of transition, for example, from the Angel stage to the Archangel stage, that is, no longer guiding a human individual but a whole group, and so forth.
13. In contrast to the false initiation of the will, Rosicrucian initiation wholly acknowledges human freedom and therefore works with the will forces in man's being not directly but through forces of the spirit (spiritual knowledge). See GA 131, 5 October 1911.
14. See S.O. Prokofieff, *May Human Beings Hear It! The Mystery of the Christmas Conference*, ch. 1, 'Rudolf Steiner's Course of Life in the Light of the Christmas Conference'.
15. What is being said here sheds a new light upon the content of Rudolf Steiner's book *Christianity as Mystical Fact and the Mysteries of Antiquity* (GA 8), at whose foundation lay a cycle of lectures that he gave in the winter of 1901/2 in Berlin. Both the content of this cycle and the book which arose from its foundation reflect precisely this aspect of the content of the Michael School—the process of transforming the old mysteries into Christianity, in which their wisdom becomes for the first time on Earth the 'mystical fact' of its entire evolution.
16. See the lecture of 18 May 1923 (GA 226).
17. Rudolf Steiner cites in this respect social threefoldness in connection with the present working amongst mankind of the Michael impulse, with which are connected also the spirits of the Third Hierarchy mentioned above who passed through his supersensible School. (See GA 223, 2 April 1923.)
18. Rudolf Steiner described in the following words this future ideal of one spiritual wisdom for all human beings as a necessary condition for the ascent of mankind to the stage of the Spirit-Self in the next cultural epoch: 'This sixth epoch will be a very important one; for it will bring peace and brotherhood through a common wisdom' (GA 103, 20 May 1908 I).
19. See the lectures of 3 June 1907 (GA 99) and 20 February 1917 (GA 175).
20. See *Occult Science* (GA 13), the chapter entitled 'Present and Future Evolution of the World and of Mankind'.
21. See further regarding this in S.O. Prokofieff, *May Human Beings Hear It! The Mystery of the Christmas Conference*, ch. 2, 'The Mystery Act of the Foundation Stone Laying on 25 December 1923'.

Bibliography

The bibliographical numbers ('GA') correspond to the series of volumes of Rudolf Steiner's complete works published by the Rudolf Steiner Nachlassverwaltung in Dornach, Switzerland. In the following list, titles of the comparable English publications containing the relevant lectures are given.

All italics in quotations derive from the present author, unless stated otherwise.

For the purposes of this English translation, quotations from Rudolf Steiner's works have—where possible—been based on published English versions and compared with the original German. The only exception to this general rule concerns quotations from the Foundation Stone Meditation, where it was considered necessary to take into account Prokofieff's Russian translations as the prime editorial guide.

GA

Books and Articles

8 *Christianity as Mystical Fact*

10 *Knowledge of the Higher Worlds*

13 *Occult Science*

26 *Anthroposophical Leading Thoughts*

Lectures

99 *Theosophy of the Rosicrucian*

102 *The Influence of Spiritual Beings upon Man*

103 *The Gospel of St. John*

130 *Esoteric Christianity and the Mission of Christian Rosenkreuz*
Faith, Love, Hope

131 *From Jesus to Christ*

145 *The Effects of Spiritual Development*

175 *Cosmic and Human Metamorphoses*

185 *From Symptom to Reality in Modern History*

223 *The Cycle of the Year as Breathing-Process of the Earth*

226 *Man's Being, his Destiny and World Evolution*

233 *World History in the Light of Anthroposophy*

233a *Rosicrucianism and Modern Initiation*
The Easter Festival Considered in Relation to the Mysteries

236 *Karmic Relationships, vol.2*

237 *Karmic Relationships, vol.3*
239 *Karmic Relationships, vols.5 and 7*
240 *Karmic Relationships, vols.6 and 8*
245 *Anweisungen für eine esoterische Schulung*
257 *Awakening to Community*
260 *The Christmas Conference Proceedings*
293 *Study of Man*

Works by Rudolf Steiner available from Rudolf Steiner Press (UK) or SteinerBooks (USA).